AF254923

# Contents

# Dedications

**My Dearest Hamdan,**

Ever since you were little, you have always asked questions about my work, trying to understand what I do for a living, and your curiosity has inspired me to create something special just for you.

This is no ordinary storybook. It gives you a peek into my work life, a fascinating field called Human Resources. Through this story, I hope to show you a small part of what I do and why it matters in a simple, fun and engaging way.

Writing this story has been an incredible experience and has allowed me to share not just the details of my job but also my passion for what I do. I believe that through this story, you will not only understand but also enjoy learning about my profession.

Lots of Love,
Your Baba Cat

# Acknowledgements

A very special thanks to my lovely wife, Noor, and my nephews, Hamdan and Mikayeel, for giving me their feedback on the initial drafts of the book. This would not have been possible without you all!

# About the Author

Qais Faisal Farooq is an Emirati HR professional with nearly two decades of experience working for several leading organisations in the UAE. He is also a former international cricketer who has proudly represented the UAE in various international tournaments.

Inspired by his inquisitive nephew, Hamdan, Qais began writing stories with the aim of helping HR professionals share their work world with their children in an engaging and relatable way.

When not working, Qais enjoys spending time with his nephews, cooking and watching movies. He believes in the power of stories to spark the imagination of young minds and create lasting memories.

# Preface

**My Fellow HR Parents,**

As HR professionals, we often find ourselves using jargon and phrases that make perfect sense in our world but are tough to explain at home, especially to kids. I wrote this storybook to bridge that gap. It all started when I tried to explain what I do for a living to my nephew, Hamdan, without overwhelming him with complex HR jargon. What began as a playful exercise turned into an idea for this storybook.

This first book, The Cookie Adventure, themed around the concept of incentives (or variable pay in our HR world), is inspired by that moment and has motivated me to continue writing to help fellow HR professionals explain what they do to their children in a simple and engaging way. This is the beginning of a series of children's books I am now working on, aimed at making our day-to-day HR experiences relatable and fun for our little ones. I hope this book and future stories I release as part of The Human Resources Chronicles allow you to share your world with your kids.

# Introducing Cookieville

Once upon a time, in a land far, far away, there was a magical kingdom called Cookieville. In Cookieville, everyone loved cookies, and the King of Cookieville, King Muffins, had the biggest cookie jar in the kingdom.

There was, however, a little problem. King Muffins wanted his cookie jar to be filled with lots of cookies, and he needed help from all the kids in Cookieville to accomplish his dream.

# The Plan: Cookie Targets

One fine morning, King Muffins called a meeting inside his mansion and said, "Kids, if we work together to fill this cookie jar, I will share cookies with everyone! But first, we need to set some targets."

The kids' eyes sparkled with excitement. "How many cookies do we need, King Muffins?" asked Hamdan, the baker's son.

"We need to fill the cookie jar with 100 cookies. That is our target," replied the King.

King Muffins then went on to explain, "If we achieve our target, each one of you will receive cookie rewards for your hard work."

The kids cheered, eager to start so they could earn their cookie rewards.

# The Challenge: Threshold Cookie Targets

"But wait," the King continued, "We need at least 45 cookies to start distributing any cookie rewards. That is our threshold. If we do not collect at least 45 cookies, there will be no cookie rewards for anyone."

The kids nodded, understanding that they had to work together to reach that first goal in order to get any cookie rewards.

# The Fun Part: Cookie Boosters

Feeling a little mischievous, King Muffins said, "If we get more than 100 cookies, you will each get extra! These are called cookie boosters. But, eating too many cookies in one go might give you kids a tummy ache or cavities in your teeth, so there is a limit, or cap, on how many extra cookies you can earn. Everyone will receive a maximum of 2 cookie boosters if we get more than 100 cookies."

The kids nodded again, understanding that eating too many cookies can give them tummy aches or cavities in their teeth.

# The Cookie Metrics: Performance Measurement

Hamdan, the baker's son, had another question. "How will we know how many and what types of cookies we need to collect?"

"We will use special cookie metrics." said the King. "We will need chocolate chip, oatmeal raisin, and sugar cookies. Each type of cookie will count towards our total, but we need at least 15 of each type to start distributing any cookie rewards."

But then, King Muffins added a twist. "We also need to count the number of sunny days we have each week; that will be another cookie metric."

Hussain, the clever boy from out of town, raised his hand. "But King Muffins, we cannot control the weather! Whether it is sunny or rainy it does not affect how many cookies we can bake or collect. It is unfair to include sunny days as a metric because we have no influence over them."

The King thought for a moment. "You know, Hussain, you make a good point. If you kids cannot influence it, it should not be a part of our metrics. Let us remove the sunny days metric and focus on what you can control: baking, growing ingredients, and decorating the cookies."

The kids were relieved, and Hamdan smiled at Hussain and said, "Good job, Hussain. That makes a lot more sense!"

# The Cookie Teams: Team Formation

The kids formed teams to bake and collect cookies. There were three teams:

The Farmers, The Bakers, and The Decorators.

- The Farmers were responsible for growing the ingredients.

- The Bakers were responsible for making delicious cookies.

- The Decorators were responsible for making the cookies look beautiful.

# The Adventure: Working Towards Cookie Targets

The kids set off on their cookie adventure. The Farmers harvested wheat and chocolate, the Bakers mixed and baked, and the Decorators added colourful sprinkles and icing.

But there was a problem. Maryam, one of the Bakers, was not very good at mixing the dough. Her cookies often turned out to be too salty or too sweet. This started to affect the total number of cookies the kids could collect.

Hamdan noticed this and decided to help. "Maryam, come and bake with me for a while, and I will show you some tricks to make the perfect cookie."

Maryam was a bit shy but agreed. Over the next few days, Hamdan patiently showed Maryam how to correctly measure ingredients and mix the dough. Mikayeel and Zayaan, from the Farmers' team, even brought her the freshest ingredients to use.

Soon, Maryam's cookies started to improve. She felt proud of her progress and was happy contributing to the team's efforts. The other kids cheered her on, and Maryam's confidence grew with every perfectly baked cookie.

# The Cookie Party: Performance Review

Finally, the big day arrived. The kids brought their cookies to the mansion and counted them. They had collected a total of 150 cookies!

King Muffins was thrilled. "You have done it! You have reached the target and even collected extra cookies, so everyone gets their cookie rewards plus the cookie boosters!"

# The Big Celebration

King Muffins threw a huge cookie party at his mansion to celebrate the success. There were chocolate chip cookies, oatmeal raisin cookies, and sugar cookies for everyone. The kids were happy and proud of their teamwork and achievement.

Cookie Party
28

# The Lesson

At the end of the party, King Muffins gathered the kids and said, "Remember, kids, when we set clear targets and work together as a team, we can achieve great things. And with a little effort, we can even get extra rewards!"

And so, the kids of Cookieville learned about rewards through their magical cookie adventure. They lived happily ever after, excited for the next challenge.

That is how King Muffins and the kids of Cookieville worked together to fill the magical cookie jar and had lots of fun along the way!

# Storybook Brief

The Cookie Adventure is a story that serves not only as a delightful read for children but also as a creative and accessible way to introduce ideas such as goal-setting, teamwork, performance management, and rewards in a manner that can resonate with young minds.